ANOTHER REASON

ANOTHER REASON

CARL DENNIS

PENGUIN POETS

PENGUIN BOOKS

Published by the Penguin Group
Penguin Group (USA) LLC
375 Hudson Street
New York, New York 10014

USA | Canada | UK | Ireland | Australia | New Zealand | India | South Africa | China
penguin.com
A Penguin Random House Company

First published in Penguin Books 2014

Cover art: *Ocean Park* #79, 1975, by Richard Diebenkorn. Oil and charcoal on canvas,
93 x 81 in. (236.2 x 205.7 cm). Estate #1495. The Richard Diebenkorn Foundation

LIBRARY OF CONGRESS CATALOGING-IN-PUBLICATION DATA
Dennis, Carl.
[Poems. Selections]
Another reason / Carl Dennis.
pages cm.—(Penguin Poets)
ISBN 978-0-14-312522-8
I. Title.
PS3554.E535A6 2014
811'.54—dc23
2013042999

Printed in the United States of America
1 3 5 7 9 10 8 6 4 2
Set in Sabon
Designed by Ginger Legato

For Emily

ACKNOWLEDGMENTS

Thanks are due to the editors of the following magazines in which some of these poems first appeared:

American Poetry Review ("Even Nietzsche," "*Job*: A New Edition," "To a Novelist," and "Words from a Poor Man")
The Atlantic Monthly ("Night Sky" and "Punch Bowl")
The Café Review ("The True Self")
The Cincinnati Review ("Birthday," "A Blessing," and "Virtue")
The Cortland Review ("From the Cove Hotel")
New Ohio Review ("At the Mall" and "Habitat")
The MacGuffin ("Angel and Cabinet Maker," "Legacy," and "Next Time")
The New Yorker ("A Maxim," "New Year's Eve," and "Unfolding")
Ploughshares ("Behind a Bookcase," "Introduction to Philosophy," and "Loitering")
Plume ("Animal Husbandry," "Missing," and "More Reason")
Provincetown Arts Magazine ("First Words")
Salmagundi ("A Clairvoyant," "In the Kingdom," "My Noah," and "Summer at the Lake")
Slate ("Silent Manners")
Upstreet ("Mailing Gifts, December 21")

This manuscript has benefited greatly from careful readings by several critical friends: Charles Altieri, Thomas Centolella, Alan Feldman, Mark Halliday, Tony Hoagland, Philip Schultz, and Emily Wheeler.

CONTENTS

I

II

III

IV

ANOTHER REASON

I

HABITAT

It's a lost cause, the effort to make heaven and hell
Eternal, undone by the very creatures
The two establishments are meant to house,
Whose natural habitat is the stream of time.
Yes, it's a comfort to hope that the good
Who are luckless here are lucky elsewhere,
That their enemies, here triumphant,
Later lose out. Let the violent suffer
A heat more fiery than the rage within them.
Let the betrayers of trust endure a chill
Even more icy than their arctic hearts.
Still, sooner or later, their victims—
The pillaged and trampled and rolled to the wall—
Safe at last in the balmy realm of the blessed,
Will grow uneasy with the thought of their oppressors
In endless torment. Sooner or later they'll decide
That the sentence already served is long enough.
No one should be surprised when Abel
Finally throws down a rope to Cain, when Jesus
Stoops to take Judas by the hand.
So hell, as imagination construes it, is doomed
To dwindle away, and then heaven as well,
As the saints return to earth to help the sinners
Learn what damage they can undo
If they give themselves to the effort,
And what damage they'll have to leave as is.

Night Sky

It's good news for the stay-at-homes like us,
The new consensus among astronomers
That the night sky appears roughly the same
From any spot in the universe,
With roughly the same number of visible stars
At similar distances, in similar congregations.
Those who've labeled the view from Earth provincial
Turn out to be mired in provincial thinking.
Look at the star map, we'll tell them. Note
How the stars have to make do without a capital,
Without a center where all roads lead, a sun
Whose pull proves irresistible to the ambitious.
And if the stars we discern above our roof
Don't seem as numerous as we've supposed them,
We'll remind ourselves of the many more
That will show themselves when the gauzy curtain
Is drawn back, the veil of dust and ash that now
Obscures their shining. Let the day draw near
When the Milky Way, visible once again
To the naked eye, inspires a silence
Appropriate to a revelation.
Nightfall then will be all that's longed for.
The morning and afternoon of a cloudless day
Will seem to pass so slowly we'll wonder
If the stars we think we remember
Are only fancies, the dust of dreams.
But no, look up. Here they are again.

AT HOME IN THE COSMOS

My friend writes with the news that the moon
Was full on the night last week when his daughter
Entered the world, a fact he might read as significant
And auspicious, he guesses, if he believed in astrology
And the universe were smaller, the Milky Way
Only a hundred stars across, not a hundred billion,
Each with a claim of influence on a birth chart.

In a smaller universe, I'll assure him,
He'd still feel inadequate to the thought
That he and Louise are responsible for the new arrival
In the borrowed cradle at the foot of their bed.
Yes, they were present at her conception,
But neither at that moment conceived of her,
And neither now has a strategy
For making her future bountiful.

In a smaller universe they would still
Give her the name of Esther in the hope
She'd prove in time to possess a few
Of dear Aunt Esther's many virtues,
As opposed to favoring poor Aunt Minerva.

A smaller universe wouldn't make it easier
For them to find the stories she needs
For inspiration, enough to outweigh
The sad examples she might be exposed to
In the yards of neighbors
Or on the buses to school or in the halls.

In my letter I'll mention my hope she becomes
The kind of girl who walks home on Fridays

From telescope night at the science museum
Entranced by the thought that the universe is too vast
To be weighed and measured, that only imagination
Can hope to embrace it, if not contain it.

And if sometimes it seems too empty for comfort,
So may her route at night from the museum.
Still, she'll have to walk it. If she's lonely,
Maybe she'll find some company in the moon
As it rises slowly above the roofs,
Alone on its sail across the sky.

SILENT MANNERS

In the book of manners that I rely on,
One chapter is devoted to keeping silent,
The one that reminds me now, as I pull off
On the shoulder of a country road to ask directions,
Not to ask the elderly man in overalls,
Who crosses the field to greet me,
Why he isn't wearing a hat on a day so sunny.
If the sun has deepened the ruts in his face,
It's too late now to stop it, the chapter reasons,
And why remind him how much he's aged?

As for the blood-vessel cobwebs beneath his eyes—
For me a sign of drinking over many years—
The same chapter warns me not to suggest,
However gently, that help is available
If he wants to stop. Who knows what escape
I might have tried if I'd had his worries:
The flooding and drought and heavy mortgage,
The money he owes the hospital, though the treatment
Failed to buy his wife an extra day.

Already I owe him something for the reticence
That keeps him from probing when I inform him
I'm on my way to visit an old friend.
He doesn't ask why I've come so seldom
That I can't recall if I'm anywhere near the turnoff.
"You can't miss it," he simply says,
"Three miles straight ahead at the stand of sweet gum."
And when my doubtful look suggests
I may find a sweet gum and never know it,
He fishes a pencil out of his bib pocket

And sketches its shape so deftly
That I'm certain I'd know it anywhere,

So deftly I need to resist the urge to ask
If he ever considered a career in art.
If he didn't, it's too late now to begin. If he did
But then decided against it, why finger that wound?

Then, before I'm tempted to ask about
The beautiful sunsets he must be able to witness
Above the hills to the west, it's time to thank him
And drive off. Why take the risk,
I hear the chapter asking, of reminding him
Of sunsets he used to watch with a companion?
Let him think of those scenes just when he chooses,
When he's in the mood for recalling
The words they used when they needed words
And the silence they liked to share.

My Noah

I can say here what I won't say openly
To you, neighbor I share a fence with:
That I'd like you to suffer a little,
Though you sign for my packages when I'm away,
To suffer for the pain I feel when arriving home
On autumn evenings to find your lawn
Bristling with signs boosting the candidates
Who proclaim all will be well when the government
Is too small to intrude on the enterprise of the busy.

To make you suffer not so much as a punishment
But as a useful lesson that intrudes for a while
On your joys as a dutiful family man, out late
Watching a night game with your two sons
Or up early to pick your wife a bouquet from the garden,
You who've proven quick, when your mother
Couldn't fend for herself in her own apartment,
To bring her home with a live-in nurse so the family
Can keep together, safe on its private ark.

I don't want your ark to spring a leak
And go down with its crew. How could I,
When I believe you'd haul me aboard
If you glimpsed me signaling from a leaky rowboat,
Me or a stranger in similar peril?
I'm thinking more of a mast-shattering storm,
One that will force you and your kin
To crowd a lifeboat in a churning sea
So you learn firsthand what it feels like
To depend on individual acts of charity.
Or maybe a lesson a little less costly
Will prove enough, a close scrape in a fog

With a floating wreck that leaves you shaken,
Spared for no reason that you can think of,
Resolved from now on to be more considerate.

Then, when your ark ran low on provisions,
I'd arrange for you to spy, near the horizon,
Poking above the flood, a hilltop
That proves to be settled by other survivors.
No docking fee required, no need for permission
To attend a meeting about the meager harvest.
Feel free to participate if someone argues
The last to find refuge here should be the first
Required to look for another settlement.
Spell out an option just as practical
In which "first" and "last" prove irrelevant,
Along with the duo of "us" and "them."

MORE REASON

Though you may be a scribe in ancient Egypt
Or a breeder of horses among the Persians,
While I'm a dry-goods merchant in Peoria, Illinois,
I'd like to believe we can sit and reason together.

Though you attended, with the flower of Athens,
The first performance of the plays of Sophocles,
While I observed one last month in modern dress
At Peoria's regional theater,
We can learn something from sharing our perspectives.

No doubt you believe in the myths that to me
Are only stories, but if I make the effort
Reason requires, I may grasp what's implied
When the hero, in serving one god, runs afoul
Of another just as imposing. Their names may be strange,
But the principles they embody may be familiar,
Two living truths locked in contention.

And if you insist that you hear a voice from above
Conversing with you in private at least once a day,
As do many of my fellow Peorians, while I hear nothing,
We can still sit down and discuss what I
Must do to live in peace with myself
And what you must do so the voice you host
Has an easier time enjoying your company.

Is your list of virtues different from mine?
That's a question we can reason about together
Over a meal we share at a kitchen table
Set anywhere between here and Persia.

You won't be offended if sincerity
Keeps me from praising the camel brisket.
I won't be offended if you fail to ask
For a second helping of rhubarb pie.

Animal Husbandry

Isn't it time to mention the millions
Of animal innocents allowed to drown
In the story of Noah, the millions sacrificed
As collateral damage when Yahweh decides
To drown mankind? Can so gross an act of injustice
Be allowed to pass without an apology?
The next edition should at least contain a chapter
On what it felt like for Noah and family
To enter, when the flood receded, a world
Of empty fields and forests, of empty sky.
And then a longer chapter on the remnant pairs
Returning to habitats devoid of their kin,
The strain of two bees trying to be a hive,
Two prairie dogs toiling to be a colony.
And consider the loneliness of the dove
Sent from the ark to scout for land
As it waited in the reeds for the ark to open.
Then imagine it darting off with its mate,
Quick to put as much distance as possible
Between them and Noah's family.
Who knows when the god of humans
Might strike out blindly again in all directions,
As if the world were to blame for his failure
To plan, on the sixth day of creation,
The last two creatures as carefully
As he planned the others. And then his failure
To observe them at least a year in the Garden
Before he urged them to fill the world.

PUNCH BOWL

The friendly way to explain the missing punch bowl
Is to assume I loaned it to someone
On a day I've forgotten, someone who,
By the time he thought of returning it,
Had lost his job and moved to another city
And loaned it to the hostess of a charity ball
Who later couldn't recall the lender's name.
As for his intention to fetch it back,
It may have been shoved aside by more pressing issues:
A sickness, say, that wouldn't ease up,
And the thought of having to face his end
With many projects left unfinished.
So the bowl sits in a bin in the charity basement,
Still waiting to be reclaimed, just like the plate
Somebody brought to a party of mine
And never retrieved. Beautiful cut glass
I've kept safe in a drawer, unused.
It would be a friendly gesture now
To lift it out of the dark, into the open.
Friendly for me to urge any guest who casts
An appreciative glance in its direction:
If it looks familiar, take it home.

LETTERS NOT WRITTEN

The letters I haven't written should be included
In any fair assessment of my accomplishments,
Like the letter telling my friend I doubt that his efforts
To enroll new voters in forgotten precincts
Will make much difference, given the money
Invested by profiteers in the status quo.
Not written and sent because doubt
Is available by the truckload, while belief
Is scarce enough to be measured in ounces
Here in a world prone to fatigue and inertia,
To whatever keeps me from bestirring myself
In causes that I admire. At least I'm ready
To honor those more active than I am.
At least I don't choose to protect myself
From painful comparisons by converting my friend
To my preference for watching from the balcony.

Or consider the letter I haven't written my niece
To inform her I think she's foolish
For spending her summer down on the Gulf,
Postponing her choice of career so she can help
In clearing a beach of tar balls from a blown well.
Not a word from me predicting the sand
Will soon be filthy again, given the sway
Of oil interests in Washington. Instead,
I'm trying to think of her as my representative,
Fulfilling our family's quota of work
For the common good so I can stay home
And write a few lines of commendation.
Here's a young woman who seems to regard

Her sacrifice as an adventure.
For her the thrill of washing an egret by hand.
For her the thrill of watching
As it stretches its wings to the wind and flies off.

ACHIEVEMENT

Though he's finished his summer job, painting houses,
Without making it clear to his companions
He won't be returning next summer as expected,
He's told his father he won't be studying medicine,
That he needs to give himself to the banjo.

As for his father, who's led a five-year study
On what appeared a breakthrough treatment for tumors,
He's willing now to admit that his final results,
However promising, are inconclusive.

And don't forget his daughter, who didn't join
Her friends when they steered their kayaks through rapids,
Who chose to sit in camp all afternoon
In the shade of poplars, eyes closed,
Listening to the rustle of leaves and grass.

And consider her mother, who's dug up the greenest lawn
In the neighborhood for a vegetable garden
From porch to curb to explore the notion
That food comes from the earth, not from the market,
Who's answered the neighbors' complaints with baskets
Of squash, tomatoes, and corn.

Also a neighbor's decision to pull up stakes,
After talking about it for years,
And begin again farther west, leaving behind
The clutter of her possessions, resolved to believe
Her new home will provide whatever she needs,
Including a rosebush under her bedroom window.

Likewise her former neighbor's resolve
To make time every evening, however busy he is,
To sit alone for an interval
Of communing with friends far off
He couldn't persuade to stay.

BIRTHDAY

Those aware of how rare it is
For a celebration to come off as planned
May be glad to learn that the birthday party
For Mary Bottsworth, age eleven,
Went off as her mother hoped it would
On Sunday, June 18, 1950,
Which means, to start with, it didn't rain
And the tables could be set outside
On the strip of grass that served as a yard.
It means Mr. Grimes wasn't out in his driveway
Tuning the moody engine of his jalopy,
That his son wasn't looking on with his radio blaring.
And the cakes Mrs. Bottsworth baked herself,
Lemon and chocolate, didn't fall as they cooled,
And the magician, whose fee pushed the cost
Of the party past the amount she'd budgeted,
Held the children's attention for almost an hour.
It means that Mary didn't look chagrined
When she opened the gifts before her guests:
A board game, a pair of kneesocks, a book, a record,
Which she later arranged on the shelf beside her bed.
Whatever tomorrow might bring, Mrs. Bottsworth
Was thankful—after the children went home
And the hard-used dishes, chipped and unchipped,
Were stacked again in the cupboard—
That the party was safely stored out of harm's way,
Ready to be called forth whenever the myth
Of a joyless childhood might need dispelling.
This day, with others like it, would prove,
When Mary looked back, that contentment,
When it happened to pass through town,

Didn't always confine itself to other houses.
Sometimes it knocked at her door, too.

FALLEN TREE

I didn't hear it falling, the tree now blocking
The trail behind the summer cabin,
Its branches tangled in the underbrush,
Its roots exposed. Did it make a sound
If no one was there to hear it? A question
That doesn't interest me now as it once did,
Fifty years ago, in freshman philosophy class—
The suggestion that the world isn't fully real
Without our participation. Now the matter at hand
Is the tree, fallen just as conclusively
As ancient Rome or Carthage.
Do I have it in me to write a brief memorial
To its meeting every challenge to its survival
Except time? Here's a chance to praise
The seed it sprang from for finding the soil
It happened to fall on an opportunity
Not to be wasted. Here's a chance to praise the sapling
It soon became for making do with the light
That managed to pierce the screen of established trees.
It must have made the most of twenty sunny summers
By the time my fellow students and I pondered the question
Of whether the sun's existence would be in jeopardy
If everyone shut his eyes at the same moment.
It's lucky someone somewhere was always peeking.
Meanwhile, the tree somehow escaped the deer
That girdled the trunks of many neighbors
When spring snows prevented the usual browsing.
Almost a miracle that the lightning strike only singed it,
That the leaf beetles stopped their feasting in time.
The wind shifted; the forest fire veered off.
The sawmill closed down a week before the loggers
Would have reached this woods, the very mill

That supplied the lumber for this summer cabin
Where I sit writing. Let these lines be my tribute
To a tree imagined just as a tree,
Not as a symbol for someone I didn't meet,
Or met once but never got to know.

II

A TEACHER

To hold on to our poems for at least a year
Before sending them off—that was one piece of advice
He gave us that we didn't pretend to follow.
It seemed to doom us to lives of waiting and tinkering.
It seemed to suggest the improvement we'd shown
In spotting problems and solving them
Still didn't mean we could trust our judgment.
Why couldn't we turn from an old-world modesty
And embrace a new-world faith that we were ready
To skipper poems crowded with images
To any shore prepared to receive them?

Of course, we took his advice not to throw out
For at least a year the poems that failed,
To keep them instead in a drawer of their own.
Maybe one day, he seemed to suggest,
A sudden upsurge of inspiration
Might wake the patient from a coma.
Only later did he seem to mean they were parts
Kept in cold storage for the unlikely chance
Of being grafted into a feeble poem
To give it more sinew, more resilience.

A poem would need to practice survival skills,
That was his message. No crowd would be waiting
Down at the dock to receive it.
For many seasons, wandering on its own,
It would have to bed down in barns and in open fields,
Under a distant sky. Only in dreams of ours
Would we have a chance to assure it
Somebody soon would make time to hear it,

Listen intently, and then, after a silent interval,
Ask for a second reading, this one more slow.

BEHIND A BOOKCASE

Behind the bookcase I moved this morning
To prepare for the plasterer, I found the book
You lent me four years ago, two years
Before your heirs sold off your library.

Did you ever wonder what had become of it,
You who lent books to so many friends
That you couldn't remember where each one went?
A book on what has to be done at once
To save the biosphere from calamity,
How best to persuade our species it's time
To think about those whose time is coming.
Four years on the floor behind the bookcase
With a congregation of dust balls and dust mites,
And with every year it's become more true.

For your sake, if not the planet's,
I ought to do more than vow
To put my copy back into circulation.
I ought at least to resist in myself
The argument spelled out in the paper today
About the need of our species to adjust
To its new environment, as the fittest
And shrewdest have always done.

For you I should join this very evening
Those who are shrewd and fit enough
Not to regard your cause as hopeless,
Not to succumb to the voice of moderation,
The fatal charm of compromise.

Near the Dig

The tribal wisdom wasn't enough
To keep the tribe from disappearing.
But if we study the potsherds and broken tools
We might learn something about living well.

The dances and songs are lost, but the evidence
From the fire pit suggests that the festivals
For planting and harvest went on for weeks,
A sign the participants were devoted
To making the most of what they had.

We can join the tribe if we're interested
In extending the rituals of the moment,
Like devoting the end of each day to watching
The sun go down with its usual flourish
Behind the garage and the lilac tree.

And then the evening ritual of describing it
In a letter to someone who wants to learn
How to be a witness, a letter in longhand
That reads as if it were written by candlelight,

As if the writer had mastered the ancient art
Of pausing now and then to admire the candle,
Its tongue of upright flame steady and silent
Above the shrinking body. It won't flare up
Even when wafer-thin, and won't hold back.

FIRST WORDS

For the first sentence of a creator,
It's hard to do better than "Let there be light."
Let there be light in the workroom
So the task of shaping a world may proceed
With no wasted effort, no guessing,
And the maker can say at the end of each day,
"This part of creation has gone as planned."

But after he rests from his six-day workout
He'll want to begin on another world,
Not settle for the job of custodian.
A world that begins this time with a different sentence
Or with no sentence at all. Does a good painter
Choose to repeat himself forever
After he makes a painting he's proud of,
Or is he eager to be adventurous?

A new creation that may not be spelled out
In terms so final, that may allow
For eons of groping before a plant
Hits on a way to use whatever sunlight
Happens to be available, before a worm
Settles into being a worm in earnest
And a bird discovers a use for feathers
Beyond its need for heating and cooling.

Some houses are made with blueprints
And some begin small, without them, and grow.
First it's a fisherman's cabin just for weekends.
Then, over decades, bedrooms are added
As needed for a growing family.
And what about a porch facing south,

And a telescope in the attic window
For scanning the stars?

And if a creator is confined to one world,
He'll want to undo it each day before dawn
So he can make it again in an instant
With his first directive, "Let there be light."
Look. Here's the new sun,
Rising the way the old one did.
Here's a new mist to be burned away.

JOB: A NEW EDITION

If we can agree to keep the kernel
And let the chaff go, I suggest, first of all,
That we cut the opening, where God agrees
To let Satan torment our hero
Merely to prove what omniscience
Must know already: that Job's devotion
Isn't dependent on his prosperity.
And how foolish it makes God look
To suppose that Satan, once proven wrong,
Will agree to forgo his spite
Against creation for even a minute.

I suggest we feature the part where Job disdains
His friends' assumption that somehow
He must be to blame for his suffering
And the part where he makes a moving appeal
To God for an explanation. I suggest we drop
God's irrelevant, angry tirade
About might and majesty versus weakness.

If the real issue is justice, our hero
Isn't impertinent for expecting his god
To practice justice as well as preach it,
For assuming the definition of justice
That holds on earth holds as well above.
Abraham isn't reproved in *Genesis*,
When God decides to burn Sodom, for asking
If it's fair to lump the good with the wicked.

In our edition let Job complain
About his treatment as long as he wants to,
For months, for decades,

And in this way secure his place forever
In the hearts of all who believe
That suffering shouldn't be silent,
That grievances ought to be aired completely,
Whether heard or not.

As for the end, if you think it's meant to suggest
That patience will be rewarded, let's cut it too.
Or at least we should add a passage
In which God, after replenishing Job's possessions,
Comes to the tent where the man sits grieving
To ask his pardon. How boorish of majesty
To have assumed that Job's new family,
New wife and children and servants,
Would be an ample substitute for the old.

A Clairvoyant

Though she charges more than the others, she's the one
To consult if you're eager to glimpse the future,
Her predictions being far more precise.
From others you'll learn that a nameless stranger
May soon do harm to somebody near you.
From her you'll learn that the fiancé
Of your sister Nancy isn't a bachelor:
That his wife is alive and well in a bungalow
Just north of Miami, with their three children.
It isn't her policy to reveal her sources.
If you don't believe her, feel free to investigate.
If she's wrong, it comes from her choosing to err
On the side of too much caution on your behalf
Rather than too little. It's easy for the negligent
To be right every time if they limit themselves
To statements too general to be useful.

Not from her the vague pronouncement
That among your many putative friends
A few may prove unreliable. She can provide you
With the names and addresses of two
Who'll soon be speaking of you in tones
Less than respectful. Whatever their motives are,
You ought to know that it won't be wise for a while
To trust the footbridge between you and them.
Better inspect the ropes for unusual wear.
And if you come to learn that her information
Doesn't fit the facts, isn't it still worth something
To be reminded that friendship requires tending?

And instead of hinting that someone you know
May soon fall ill, which you've guessed already,

She'll tell you the chest cold annoying Victor,
Your oldest friend, will soon become pneumonia,
Though he'll try to conceal it as long as he can.
Maybe his notions of dignity demand it.
Or maybe he wants to spare you his fears.
Will you bear her a grudge for ranking
Your right to know higher than his right to privacy?
And if you later learn that his health is really
As good as yours, will you ask for a refund
Or will you thank her, as you should,
For her reminder that his years are numbered?
Faithful Victor, who so far hasn't been told
How much his letters have meant to you, his visits,
His calls when he hasn't heard from you for a while.

A GIFT FROM WALES

Having lingered, on my first trip to Europe, longer
In Paris than I expected, I had to forgo
Walking in Wales. But that didn't keep me
From becoming deeply indebted to Wales
When I phoned the hotel in Cardiff
To cancel my reservation and save my deposit.
"There's a letter for you," the desk clerk said
In a rich contralto. "Would you like us to send it on?"
"Better read it to me, if you have time,
Since I keep moving." And that's how it happened
I heard, as I sat in a booth at the Gare du Nord,
Awaiting the train to Brussels, my mother's sentences,
Penned in Missouri, delivered with Welsh intonations.
That's how her usual mix of family news,
Tips about healthy eating, and encouragement
To visit any noteworthy local garden
Took on an undercurrent of mystery.
That's why they seemed imbued with the suggestion
My travels were more than a summer's entertainment,
Were in fact a quest for something just as meaningful
As whatever a knight went searching for
When he rode out from a castle in Wales.
Some truth more practical than a grail
And more surprising would soon be mine
Once I learned to listen to people whose words
I regarded before as predictable and forgettable.
And I had questions about the desk clerk,
Who'd read the letter as if she'd composed it herself,
Inspired by a sincere concern for my well-being.
What did it mean, her convincing performance?
If it wasn't part of her job at the hotel,

Was it part of some other calling
Defined in a legend I didn't know yet
But would want to learn if the chance were offered?

FROM THE COVE HOTEL

If you value justice, you'll want to choose our hotel,
Though it's ranked only fourth best
Among the dozen hotels on the bay
And its rates are those of the one ranked first.
Justice because we pay our workers
More nearly what they deserve, which is almost twice
The salaries others offer. That's the reason
We can't afford the extra help required
To keep the kitchen open for late-night orders.
That's why if you need extra towels after five p.m.,
When the housekeeping staff goes home,
You're invited to help yourself from the linen closet
By the vending machines on the second floor.
That's why there isn't a gym or a steam room.
And all the money we save by our location
(Half a mile from the beach) in beachfront taxes
Is passed on to the people who serve you
With care, with courtesy. Are you ready to help them
By taking in stride an easy, ten-minute walk
Past the modest storefronts where they tend to shop
To a beach as clean as the beaches of hotels
Where a walk from room to ocean takes ten seconds?
Wouldn't you say there's something a little desperate
About people whose craving for pleasure is so intense
They haven't a moment to observe the world
Our workers dwell in as they earn a living
Ample enough for them to afford a few expenses
Beyond necessities? We're proud that our cook
Manages to support his daughter in law school.
The young woman's so grateful we pay her father
More than the market calls for that she intends

To advise her clients to focus first
On the option of settling out of court
By appealing to a natural sense of fairness.
It's in that spirit we appeal to yours.

In the Kingdom

Once in a great while I come upon them,
Inhabitants of the kingdom of the leisurely,
Like the two I happened upon last week
Standing in the museum before a van Gogh:
A woman in her early thirties, a boy about ten,
Dressed casually and speaking softly
With local inflections, who didn't move
While I made a circuit of the big room
In twenty minutes. There they were,
Just where I'd left them, absorbed in *The Drinkers*,
In which three men stand at a table in a field,
Each tilting back a glass of wine while a child
Off to the side, barely as tall as the table,
Drinks from a glass of milk he holds with both hands.

Once in a while choosing to listen in unnoticed
Doesn't seem unmannerly. So I stood behind them
While the woman gently posed questions,
As if half to herself, and the boy
Answered eagerly as best he could.
Do the men look the same age or different?
Would you say they're really three men
Or one man at different times of his life?
Is the child, do you think, his son,
Or the boy that the man once was
Decades before? And I felt I knew
Where her questions were heading.
Soon she would ask if anyone in the painting
Looked as if his thirst was being satisfied,

And if not, are there any clues why?
And then the question, what do we really thirst for,
And how should we look for it, and where?

All it seemed I needed to do was wait,
And she, though half my age, would lead me
Along a path that ended in revelation.
Or maybe the concept of path isn't appropriate
For the kingdom of the leisurely. Maybe for them
Their conversation wasn't a wayside marker.
They may have felt they'd come to the very spot
Where they wanted to be and were doing
Just what they'd hoped to do, as if fishing
Together at their favorite creek, or rambling
Down to a beach to gather seaweed, or returning
To make a broth they might have been willing
To share with me if I had asked them.
But I'd taken enough already,
Enough for someone who had an appointment
Later that afternoon in the kingdom of the busy,
One I could keep if I stayed to listen
Only a moment more.

Words from a Poor Man

You'd like to believe that wanting the best for yourself
Means wanting the best for me as well.
But so far, to judge by your actions,
It seems to mean you want me to be as happy
In my two cramped rooms by the dock
As you are in your spacious house by the golf course.
You'd like me to feel the meagerness of my window light
Far less than you would and to be untroubled
By noise and odors you'd find offensive.
You want me to like my job—cleaning
The big boats after weekend jaunts—
Enough that I don't feel aggrieved,
After I've paid my rent and bought my groceries,
To find my bank balance shrunk to zero.
If I can imagine lives beyond my reach,
You hope I can rise above resentment to a lofty
Tranquillity of the spirit you couldn't manage
So the long list of missed opportunities
Isn't a heavy chain dragging me down.
If my future doesn't beckon, you hope my present
Seems inviting enough: that I'm someone
Who doesn't require a cloudless sky
To enjoy a picnic. Rain in the afternoon
Means little to me, you want to believe,
The annoyance of a damp blanket,
While to you, accustomed as you are
To exerting your will in small matters
As well as large, it would be an injury.

To a Novelist

I'll turn to our differences in a moment,
But I'd like to begin by saying I share
Your deep suspicion of general statements,
Your reluctance to name, for example,
One trait everyone needs if he wants to be happy.
I admire your focus wholly on instances,
On a cluster of characters, say, crowding the entrance
Of Kensington High School on a rainy evening.
In fifteen minutes a meeting begins in the gym
For those with strong opinions about the mall
Now in the planning stage for the outskirts.
I like how you call from the crowd a developer
To give an impassioned speech urging the town
Not to stand in the way of progress. I like the rebuttal
You assign to a local merchant, his warning that one by one
The stores in the center of town will go dark.
And when a woman in a business suit
Speaks of the need for one-stop indoor shopping
In the dead of winter, another wearing a Rembrandt hat
Speaks of the need for people to meet in stores
Where they used to meet as children. "The affections,"
She says in closing, "if they're to leaf out and bloom,
Must root themselves in the soil of the familiar."
I can see you pausing to write in the margin,
"Too formal, too flowery," a note to yourself
So your next draft proves credible line by line.
But here in the first draft it's best to embrace momentum,
To let this woman, who may turn out to be your heroine,
Be approached by a man who may be your hero
And asked if she's free to explore over coffee
The implications of her organic metaphor.
And I admire how, in the coffee shop,

You enlarge with a few examples on the theme
Of how people often fail to recognize
Happiness when it's offered. It's sad
That the woman's boss at the restaurant
Where she's the chef is a restless man
Who can't take pleasure in his achievement—
A budget bistro with lofty standards.
It's sad that the hero's former sweetheart,
Whose gloom appealed to his need to be a rescuer,
Proved in the end impervious to his efforts.
Two strangers, but already I feel engaged
Enough to want the exchange to unfold
Toward an insight that leaves them both
With a better grasp of how much they've received
Beyond their due or how much they're missing.
And that's where you and I part company.
To you, it seems, they've spoken enough
After a few exchanges to get the novel moving.
Time now for them to return to their lives.
So there they stand, outside the coffee shop,
Shaking hands in the rain as the plot requires,
The relentless plot waiting in ambush
To test their resolve in the coming chapters.
How quiet it is at the table they've left,
Where even now they might be approaching clarity
If you'd been willing to let them stay.

EVEN NIETZSCHE

Even Nietzsche, who regarded benevolence
As the first temptation, wanted to help his readers,
Not leave them stymied. First to undo their faith
In the old law and the new. Then to ask each
To come up with a law of his own devising
That required obedience to himself.

Sick in body, he wanted his readers to be robust.
Vexed in spirit, he wanted them to achieve serenity.
The day he collapsed on the street while running
To stop a hackney driver from beating his horse
He may have intended not only to shield the horse
But to show the driver that giving pain
Isn't the only way to feel powerful.

Don't waste your strength, he hoped to tell him,
On resenting your customers for making you wait
In the rain today. Learn to watch their antics
From a seat in the balcony while you endow
Your part in the play with grace, with style.

So Nietzsche tried to observe himself
Playing the part of prophet with gusto
Even when no one noticed he'd smashed the idols
That cast their shadow on earthly life,
When no one thanked him for his years of breathing
The acrid dust clouds of dogma shards.

At the end, when he called himself "the Antichrist,"
It's possible that behind the self-inflation
He may have been mocking himself

For preaching a gospel that drew no crowds,
That won him no disciples.

It must have been hard for him to preserve his faith
That readers to come, in times more friendly,
Would think of him as their benefactor.
But he had to try. Not for him,
If he could help it, the killjoy suspicion
That a prophet's toil wasn't worth the trouble,
That a shrewder man would have chosen a softer trade.

ANGEL AND CABINETMAKER

No doubt the angel who hoped to guide a prophet
Was disappointed when assigned to you,
You whose gift for working with crowds was small
Compared to your gift for working with wood.
No doubt your apprenticeship in your uncle's workshop
Must have seemed to her lacking in incident
Compared to the trials of a young prophet
Whose sermons are mocked for their earnestness.
Still she worked to inspire in you the patience
To submit to your uncle's rules, to limit yourself
For years to making bookcases and hat racks.

And later, when you were a journeyman,
She helped to inspire in you the confidence
That led to your breakthrough design for a credenza
Lighter and airier than many in fashion,
Though just as sturdy. No loss to you if she dreamed
Now and then of helping a prophet stand tall
When accused of inciting unrest in the lowly,
Of persuading the last they deserved to be first.

She never failed you in your dark hour
When the demand for your handiwork shrank to zero,
Never ceased to assure you your time was coming.
So don't be hurt if she dreamed of visiting
The barred cell of a prophet as he waited alone
To be tried for refusing an ultimatum:
Either leave the city or stay and keep quiet.

Be strong, be true, she'd have told him
On the day of his sentence and execution,
Had she been assigned him. And later,

She'd have tried to protect his message
From being obscured or coarsened. Still,
In the role assigned her, she'll do her best,
After you leave the scene, to collect a few
Extant examples of your handiwork—
Tables, sideboards, chests of drawers—
From garage sales and attics, and make them available
As useful examples for craftsmen to come.

It shouldn't be hard to find some, given how many
You'll have made in the hope that a few
Would be recognized by the world as timeless.
And if your name is forgotten, she'll use that loss
To appeal to journeymen to be less concerned
With reputation and more with process.
Now the early pleasure of selecting the wood
Fresh from the sawmill; now the final pleasure
Of rubbing the varnish till it shines.

III

POINT OF VIEW

From the general point of view, my health
Is no more significant than the health of others,
But from the personal, there's no comparison.
The pain in my side as I climb the trail
To the wooded campsite fills the foreground
Of my attention with a vivid flame,
While the pain of others is rumor only,
A gray smudge far in the hazy distance.

From the general point of view, my one task
Is to leave the campsite as it would be left
By anyone concerned with the general welfare:
With the trash deposited in the trash pit,
The kindling neatly stacked in the lean-to.
But my one task from the personal point of view
Is deciding whether hiking will bring me
The satisfaction I need the most,
Or birding, or fishing—adventures that end
With a climb at sunset to enjoy the vista.

What makes the sunset remarkable for anyone
Ready to witness it—that's the issue
The general point of view delights in exploring.
But from the personal, the issue is how to persuade
The few who occupy my favorite lookout
That it behooves them, now that I've come,
To surrender their spot to me.
Against their claim of priority, my deeper claim
That my need for beauty is boundless
While theirs is measured, modest, small.

BASEMENT

I could never do what he did,
The man who gave up a chance for a family
And a career in order to care
For his bedridden aunt, but at least
I can acknowledge his sacrifice.
At least I don't tell myself that if the choice
Was really his own, and he didn't regret it,
He was merely pursuing happiness as he defined it,
Just like everyone else on the planet.

To reason like that would betoken a grudging spirit,
Whereas I intend to be ready with praise
Not only for rare conduct like his but for the kind
Exemplified by the favor a couple I know
Did for a carpenter without a workshop
By letting him use their basement.
Plenty of room, they told themselves,
For his workbench and lathe, jigsaw and circle saw,
Without intruding on their laundry room
Or the corner they reserved for garden tools.

A basement little used, like mine,
By two who decided that whatever intentions
They might have harbored twenty years back
For a game room or craft room were now just cobwebs,
Waiting to be brushed aside by an act of goodwill
That would cost them nothing, or next to nothing,
And prove a godsend to someone else.

Two writers who may have figured that any noise
Drifting up the stairs to their attic studies,
Any faint humming and hammering,

Might do them good. Though they wanted their thoughts
To be safe from the ebb and flow of opinion
Down on the street, they wanted their words
To be useful to someone below
Doing the practical work of the world.

They weren't troubled by a fear like mine,
That if I acted like them I'd wake up one morning
Feeling I'd been imposed on,
Regretting my yielding in a weak moment
To a voice that wasn't really my own
But that of somebody far more sociable,
Convinced I'd prove an eager recruit.
Why not resist him now, I reasoned,
And spare him, later, the pain
Of having to recognize his mistake.

THE TRUE SELF

You have to keep alert if you want to distinguish
Between a man giving by nature
And a man selfish by nature
Who'd like to become more giving.

Both men volunteer to work one night a week
In the kitchen at Loaves and Fishes,
Dishing out tuna casserole to the regulars.

For the one giving by nature, it's a pleasure
To help in a task where there's no delay
Between wish and accomplishment.
For the one selfish by nature, it's a pleasure
To behave all evening like someone else.

Here comes one of them back from a walk
To the farthest grocery, the only store
Supplied by growers fair to their pickers.
Is it the giving one, eager to help the deserving,
Or the selfish one, who hopes to become,
With practice, more moved by the thought
Of acting justly than he's been so far,
To find it congenial, not merely proper?

To guess who's who, you have to notice
Which one needs a nap in the afternoon,
A sign of the extra work required
To learn the lines of a part that feels unnatural.
And then the work of speaking
With such conviction that even he
Will be uncertain he can tell the difference

Between the man he's playing
And the man he is.

SUMMER AT THE LAKE

Let's not argue today about the temperature
Of the wind that's blowing across the lake.
Let's agree that for me it's warm,
Given the genes I may have inherited
From forebears who hailed from Lapland,
While for you, given what may have been
Your tropical bloodlines, it's chilly.
I'll be back in a minute with your sweater.

As for the man far out in a rowboat,
Let's agree that for me he appears
Happy to be alone with his thoughts,
Enjoying the kind of solitude I longed for
During my boyhood in a crowded flat,
While for you, given your girlhood
On a lonely farm in Nebraska,
He seems to be aching for a friend.

Who's right isn't the issue before us,
Whose map provides the truest account of the shoreline.
We're not on a sloop hoping to reach a cove
Before the storm hits. We're in a kitchen
Preparing a dish that lets us combine
Our favorite ingredients. Instead of two apples,
The piquant duo of mango and onion.

If you don't like my metaphors, you can offer your own
While we stroll this evening along the lakeshore.
I'd like to elaborate on my sense, when a boy,
That the waves were making an effort to speak,
Repeating one word again and again.
You can elaborate on your sense, when a girl,

That they could have spoken more clearly
If they'd wanted others to understand them.

By the time we get back to the cabin,
The first stars should be glimmering.
Time for me to regret they aren't closer,
So any blessings they shower on us
Would have a better chance of falling on target.
Time for you to regret they aren't more distant,
So you could be more confident that their influence
Is too faint down here to make a difference.

AT THE MALL

It's a long time now since the beech tree
That you and Martha Spicer inscribed
With your twined initials was reduced to flooring
For houses later pulled down to make way
For the Northtown Mall, the very mall
Where you take your walk on rainy mornings.
In a few more weeks of the exercise program
Prescribed by your doctor, you should feel
Nearly as strong as you felt before your rib cage
Was slit and opened for a triple bypass.
Then you'll confront the years still left you
With the zeal they merit, or the fortitude.
Be sure you're in line when the mall doors open,
Before the aisles fill with serious shoppers
Intent on finding items more sturdy
Than their bodies are proving to be.
Could Martha Spicer be among them?
What you felt for each other back then
Didn't survive the separation of college,
Though now it seems careless of you
Not to have kept in touch. Maybe you've passed her
Unrecognized as she's looked for outfits
Suitable for the climate of her next adventure—
Greenland in spring, say, or autumn in Madagascar—
Or looked for gifts to make her grandchildren
Curious about the world they live in,
A book, for instance, devoted to local trees.
On the cover, a towering beech stands resplendent,
The very kind she carved her initials in long ago
With a boy whose name may be resting now
On the tip of her tongue, or almost resting.
If she can't quite recall it, it needn't mean

The ritual didn't matter to her,
Just that other events have come along
To overlay the impression.
All the more reason for you, now that your days
Allow you an ample margin,
To take up the work of remembering
Who the young ones were on the day
They decided the tree should testify
That they passed its way once, side by side.

The Odds

You may be right about how long the odds are
We'll be together ten years from now,
Given how fluid our moods are,
How fickle our memories.
But our chances are good compared
To the odds we've beaten just to be here:
The odds against life as we know it
Emerging on any planet; the meager odds
That on this planet third from the sun,
One of its many improbable species
Would master the art of using pronouns.

I take your point that when we refer
To "you" and "I" ten years from now
We may be referring to people who differ
From us so much that they won't be versions
Of who we are but separate beings
Unknown to us. Is an old sickle
With a new blade, with a solid handle
Replacing a cracked original,
A different sickle or the same sickle
Wholly repaired? That's a question
Whoever we'll be ten years from now
May still be asking while cutting the weeds
That narrow the walk from porch to curb
Or obscure the borders of the patio.

Maybe the people we'll be ten years from now
Will turn from the path they share to follow
Separate branches for reasons as strange
To us, if we could guess them, as the reasons
Our galaxy has been pushing out untethered

For eons toward the edge of nothing.
Still, nothing prevents us now from trying
To live one of the days left us to share
As we believe it ought to be lived.
Even a day like this one—
When all we've planned is a stroll
Out on the causeway to Bird Island—
Could be a candidate. A day we may want
To add to those we'd be glad to live
Again as often as the odds allow us
A sliver of possibility, a list
That will serve as our version of forever.

MAILING GIFTS, DECEMBER 21

I wouldn't be fretting about the extra minutes
The slow clerk at window three is making me wait
If I were more in harmony with the Christmas spirit,
Prepared to feel for an hour the flow of fellowship
That a saint is prepared to feel all year.

After all, now that I'm close enough to listen in,
It's clear he isn't staging a private slowdown
To vex the management, as I thought at first,
Or to punish his customers for waiting
Till Christmas week to send their gifts off.
No. The problem appears to be his courtesy,
His refusal to rush his explanations,
To stint even one of the options for shipping.

If I were a saint, I would think of myself
As fortunate to be standing just where I am,
With a good view of the attention he's paying
To the gray-haired wife and husband
Now informing him that the big box
They've heaved to the counter contains a tricycle
For their sensitive grandson Herbert,
A sweet-tempered five-year-old, but sickly,
Who could use more exercise in the sun.

To watch the clerk behaving as if these two
Were his only customers of the day
Would suggest to me, if I were a saint,
That he's one of the wise men,
Confident that the dispensation of time
Has been set aside for one more generous.
But to me as I am he seems oblivious,

Unaware he's an accomplice in a robbery
That leaves me without the leisure I've promised others.

A clerk without common sense now increasing my loss
By accepting the photograph of the boy
That the couple hands him and holding it up
To the light to study it. But if I were a saint,
I'd feel blessed to witness his sober appreciation.
And I might decide to embrace his example,
Loyal for life to a modest master
Who'd never suppose he had a disciple,
Never presume he taught me anything.

To Taste

I wish I could persuade you to hesitate
For just a moment between observing and judging,
To trust a little less in appearances.
As soon as you note that the woman
Seated across the table at the dinner party
Is wearing a heavy ring on each finger,
You boldly assign her a failing grade in style
And turn away. Never mind circumstances;
Never mind explanations.

To you it's beside the point to wonder
Whether she grew up in a family so poor
That she needs reminding her years of privation
Are far behind her. It's beside the point
To ask if she's lavishing rings on herself
In an effort to compensate for something essential
That her parents hadn't enough to spare.

As for treating her parents fairly,
The issue is light-years beyond your focus,
Though the woman herself may have toiled for decades
To recognize that her mother and father
Grew up in households that left them fearful,
That they passed their fears on despite themselves
To the daughter they wished the best for.

A fearful woman, perhaps, whose rings assist her
As dependable charms when she ventures alone
Down a path that to her seems dark and haunted.
Not one ring, she's certain, is unhappy it's hers.
Not one is itching to leave. So how,
I would ask you, Taste, if you cared to listen,

Could she leave even one behind
When she drove to dinner this evening?
How indulge in the game of playing favorites?

To Reason

It wouldn't be fair to blame you for the wrongs
Done in your name, as they're done in the name
Of god or country, peace or freedom.

Not fair to ignore the gift you bring to all
Who try to serve you: a truth beyond the senses.
For you it's obvious that the hungry of Madagascar

Are just as needy as the hungry at home.
And when the issues are local, you're the one
Determined to give all sides a hearing.

It's you, at the public meeting about the wisdom
Of damming the river, who are open both to the call
Of cities downriver for flood protection

And to the protest of a village that may soon
Be turned into lake bed. The claims of both parties
Have merit: the argument that the needs of the many

Ought to be satisfied, and the argument
That the rights of the few must be respected,
That justice is more than a matter of numbers.

You make it clear to the voters that their decision,
However enlightened, should still be painful. And if most
Vote for the dam, you do your best to remind them

That the new village planned for the dispossessed
On higher ground isn't superior to the old,
Though it's brick, not clapboard, with wider streets.

And you won't try to convince the people in mourning
For the village soon to be abandoned that change,
When justified, always means progress.

You won't suggest to them that becoming wise
Requires forgetting the houses they can't return to,
The streets they could count on to lead them home.

VIRTUE

Because it's harder for me to be generous
Than it is for you, I can rightly claim
To be more virtuous than you are
When I'm successful. For virtue is less
A matter of yielding to one's inclinations
Than of stout resistance for a larger purpose.
For you it's natural to be attentive if someone
Takes you aside to unfold a story of hardship.
It's natural for you to respond with sympathy.
For me it's all I can do not to break in
With proof my troubles are more significant.
As soon as I'm done with my quota of listening,
I make my excuses and take my leave,
While you remain just where you are,
All ears for a speaker who's swept along
On a flood of grievance, as if whatever
You planned for today can be done tomorrow
Just as well, or as if whatever is left undone
In this life can be done in the next.
Or do you imagine you got your fill
In a prior existence of telling your story
And now can embrace the role of confidante?
No wonder patience is harder for me,
A nonbeliever who's sadly certain
This life is the only life he'll be offered.
That's why my single hour of listening
Displays more virtue than weeks of yours.
Lucky for you I don't require virtue
In all my companions. A few intrigue me
For being born in uplands that others

Can reach, if ever, only by years of climbing.
Free of that labor, you should try to admire
Those who must face it. Why not begin with me?

A BLESSING

To be able to trust your eyes—that's a great blessing.
To believe that the pane of glass in your upstairs window
Is in fact transparent, that the narrow,
Winding streets seeming to lie beyond it
Are not a reflection of something narrow
And dark within you, just a winding passage
That will lead, eventually, to an open square.
To believe you're entitled, when you reach it,
To sit on a bench in the sun by the marble fountain,
That you haven't come to envy the beautiful,
To belittle it, to despoil it. No.
You're here to muse on the possibility
It can serve you as an example,
As a lesson in taking pleasure in what you are,
In giving pleasure by not withholding.
Maybe this gracious self is the person
Your friends have noticed from the beginning.
Your inability to observe it so far
Needn't mean they're deluded, just that their distance
Provides them the chance to see you whole.
Maybe whatever you need to do
To deserve their loyalty you've done already.
If you then do more, it could mean your heart
Has committed itself to overflowing
And you've chosen to let it have its way.

MEANING

If a life needn't be useful to be meaningful,
Then maybe a life of sunbathing on a beach
Can be thought of as meaningful for at least a few,
The few, say, who view the sun as a god
And consider basking a form of worship.

As for those devoted to partnership with a surfboard
Or a pair of ice skates or a bag of golf clubs,
Though I can't argue their lives are useful,
I'd be reluctant to claim they have no meaning
Even if no one observes their display of mastery.

No one is listening to the librarian
I can call to mind as she practices, after work,
In her flat on Hoover Street, the viola da gamba
In the one hour of day that for her is golden.
So what if she'll never be good enough
To give a concert people will pay to hear?

When I need to think of her with an audience,
I can imagine the ghosts of composers dead for centuries
Pleased to hear her doing her best with their music.

And isn't it pleasing, as we walk at dusk to our cars
Parked on Hoover Street, after a meeting
On saving a shuttered hotel from the wrecking ball,
To catch the sound of someone filling a room
We won't be visiting with a haunting solo?

And then the gifts we receive by imagining
How down at the beach today surfers made sure
The big waves we weren't there to appreciate

Didn't go begging for attention.
And think of the sunlight we failed to welcome,
How others stepped forward to take it in.

Next Time

Just because we failed on the first try,
And the second, to be happy together, doesn't mean
We'll fail on the third if we learn from our errors.

Think of us as two travelers who resolve next time
To choose a campsite closer to a creek or lake
So we needn't worry when drinking deep.

And next time let's try to camp near a woods
So we don't waste an afternoon gathering fuel
When we could be gathering nuts and berries.

And let's wait longer before deciding to make
Our camp a homestead, to pass a year
Without once feeling the urge to move on.

And when the spot proves truly congenial,
Let's not lament that we didn't come earlier,
That we barely have time now to cut the logs

For our starter cabin and roof the walls
And dig our garden and plant the saplings
Whose growth we won't be here to admire.

Free of a past we haven't shared
And a future we won't, we'll devote ourselves
To making the present feel so valued

It will want to linger with us far longer
Than time permits it. Why move on
When no welcome to come will outdo ours?

LOITERING

"No Loitering" reads the sign by the school.
But what about a school that offers courses
In loitering as an art, each class designed
To break another link in the argument
That we ought to be somewhere else by nightfall,
Ought to start now if we're to arrive on time
For the meeting of those in need of a truth
We've distilled over years in private study.
It's likely they know already what we know.
Better stay here, loitering at dusk in the garden
A moment more, while the resident birds and squirrels
Settle themselves in the boughs of the linden,
And the roiled thoughts of the day grow quiet.
This is the hour when the lover loiters on the sidewalk
Across the street from his sweetheart's house,
Waiting to see a light go on in her study
So he can imagine her reading his letter
In a mood that prompts her to a kind reply.
This is the hour when a daughter loiters
By her mother's grave, in the final moments
Before the gate of the graveyard is locked for the night.
Here's a last chance for her mother's spirit
To make its presence felt unmistakably.
Gone to a better world, the minister said.
But her mother wasn't looking for an alternative.
How happy she would have been to loiter in this one
An extra summer, plus an extra day.

IV

A MAXIM

To live each day as if it might be the last
Is an injunction that Marcus Aurelius
Inscribes in his journal to remind himself
That he, too, however privileged, is mortal,
That whatever bounty is destined to reach him
Has reached him already, many times.
But if you take his maxim too literally
And devote your mornings to tinkering with your will,
Your afternoons and evenings to saying farewell
To friends and family, you'll come to regret it.
Soon your lawyer won't fit you into his schedule.
Soon your dear ones will hide in a closet
When they hear your heavy step on the porch.
And then your house will slide into disrepair.
If this is my last day, you'll say to yourself,
Why waste time sealing drafts in the window frames
Or cleaning gutters or patching the driveway?
If you don't want your heirs to curse the day
You first opened Marcus's journals,
Take him simply to mean you should find an hour
Each day to pay a debt or forgive one,
To write a letter of thanks or apology.
No shame in leaving behind some evidence
You were hoping to live beyond the moment.
No shame in a ticket to a concert seven months off,
Or, better yet, two tickets, as if you were hoping
To meet by then someone who'd love to join you,
Two seats near the front so you catch each note.

LEGACY

If I'm not leaving a gift behind
That many may profit from,
I may be leaving a gift for a few.
Or if not a gift exactly, then a gap
In the hearts of the two or three
Who may consider me irreplaceable.

But do I really want my beloved few
To suffer a wound that closes slowly
And leaves a scar?
Better to wish that they carry with them
A part of me they can turn to
When the need arises, a reedy voice
That offers the kind of encouragement
Or consolation I might have offered.

Or if not a voice, then at least an image
Floating up from the void when summoned,
Like those that have often succored me.
Burton doesn't speak in my dreams
Any longer, but I can picture him still
Writing in the margins of the book he's reading,
Heartened to find an author bold enough
To back a truth nobody wants to hear.

Ginny, always more quiet, would let me
Even in dreams do most of the talking.
But I can see her still crossing a room
To speak to a guest outside the circle
Of easy banter. I can make out her eager look

That has little to do with duty and much
With an openness to discovery.

Burton, what are you reading these days?—
That's a question I'd like to ask.
How do you think the cause of truth is faring?
Ginny, which among those at the margins
Would you recommend approaching first?
And do either of you have a question you'd ask
For my sake if you were able, one you'd advise me
Not to put off for some other day?

MISSING

If I told you simply that the bed in the Baptist hospital
Last occupied by Cora Stokes is empty again,
And the patient didn't go home, you'd be likely
Not to feel much interest. So I'm adding here
My news that she's gone missing, that any tip
On her whereabouts will be highly prized.
Cora Stokes, female, African American,
Forty-seven, five feet five inches,
Slender, with a mole on her chin
And a small scar over her right eyebrow.
Last seen the day before yesterday
In the cardiac wing by a night nurse
Who didn't like the looks of her chart.
Till a week ago, a teacher of botany
At Jefferson Junior High in Chesterfield.
On Wednesday nights a player of bridge
With three women she's known since grade school.
Left-handed. Slaps her head with her left hand
When she makes a mistake in bidding
Made by beginners. Owner of a bungalow
On Cherry Street, three bedrooms,
One occupied by her mother, Bessie,
Seventy-six, crippled by arthritis,
One by her daughter, Trish, eleven,
A fifth grader at Holy Angels, no Baptist school
Nearby being available. Single mother
Observed by neighbors on weekends
Working with daughter in vegetable garden
While mother looks on from a canvas chair.
Observed on Sundays driving the pair
To Second Baptist on Randolph Street.
Believes that her god sees everything;

Not sure what he does with the information.
An abstainer from alcohol for eleven years,
Except for the break after the operation
When a lump in her right breast was removed.
Moviegoer, with a preference for heavy
Domestic drama, three-handkerchief features
That serve to keep her heart soft and flexible.
Annoyed she can't be more patient
With two backbiting colleagues,
Two teachers she'd assign some serious time
In Purgatory if she were Catholic.
Reader of the personal columns in the *Star*,
Confident she'll be happier when she swears off men
And doesn't relent as she did the last time.
Lover of swing band music. Owner of a canary
She gives the run of the house for an hour at dusk,
The time of day that for her seems least confining,
Most open to possibility, to change.
No information you offer is likely to change
The case enough, I realize, to lead
To her being found, but if you open yourself
To the search a moment, her friends
Will consider themselves in debt to you
For a sum that they can't repay.

UNFOLDING

If there is no spirit unfolding itself in history,
No gradual growth of consciousness
Beneath the landgrabs and forced migrations,
The bought elections, the betrayal of trust
By party factions in the name of progress—
What about spirit in the personal realm
Unfolding slowly inside us, so slowly
That our best days seem like a holding action?
Seasons repeat themselves, but the tree
Shading the yard keeps growing.
Don't be chagrined that the sadness you felt
This evening beside the bed of a friend
Whose strength is ebbing wasn't more profound
Than the sadness of yesterday, that you still
Can't imagine a fraction of what he's feeling
As the world he loves slips from his grasp.
No progress from your perspective,
But who's to say what you might notice
If the scroll of the last few months were unrolled
On the table before you, how clear it might be
That your understanding of all you're losing
In losing him has been slowly deepening?
Another day, you say to yourself at dusk
As you climb your porch steps, which you notice
Could use some scraping and painting this weekend,
A fresh coat that with luck will last a year.

INTRODUCTION TO PHILOSOPHY

Near the end of the course, in that part of the hour
Reserved for questions, a silence fell on the class
When the girl who'd been quiet all semester
Raised her hand to ask if anyone there besides her
Believed in heaven. An embarrassed silence
While each of us wondered why she hadn't chosen
To go to the Bible college just a mile away.
Or if not heaven, she added after a moment,
Did any of us believe the unlucky were granted
A second life on earth, under stars more friendly?
If not, what did we tell ourselves
When facing the fact of unequal portions?
How did we deal with the students in the flat above,
Who died in the fire that somehow missed us,
With the family crushed by the truck
That failed to stop at the corner we'd passed
A moment before? And what about those
Whose particular stories are lost
In a shared disaster, inhabitants of a town
Flattened by a tsunami or buried in a mudslide
Or torched by a warlord eager to prove
That the ruthless can always defeat the peaceable?
What truth did we lean on, she wondered,
That might steady her too if her faith
Should happen to stumble? Then she was done,
Leaving us with a silence that had no trouble
Stretching to fill the hour and lingering
As we pulled our coats on and ventured out
To see if our luck would hold all day.

New Year's Eve

However busy you are, you should still reserve
One evening a year for thinking about your double,
The man who took the curve on Conway Road
Too fast, given the icy patches that night,
But no faster than you did; the man whose car,
When it slid through the shoulder,
Happened to strike a girl walking alone
From a neighbor's party to her parents' farm,
While your car struck nothing more notable
Than a snowbank.

One evening for recalling how soon you transformed
Your accident into a comic tale
Told first at a body shop, for comparing
That hour of pleasure with his hour of pain
At the house of the stricken parents, and his many
Long afternoons at the Lutheran graveyard.

It's only human of you to assume your luck
Has something to do with your character.
Just don't be surprised if he considers
The misfortune he's suffered somehow deserved,
A portion of grief justly imposed.

Lucky you, whose personal faith has widened
To include an angel assigned to protect you
From the usual outcome of heedless moments.
But this evening consider the angel he lives with,
The stern enforcer who drives the sinners
Out of the Garden with a flaming sword
And locks the gate.

WORDS FROM JOHN

I know you'll want to describe in your poem
How full the pews were at my funeral service,
Full of people I was able to give some hope
About their addictions when no one else could.
You'll want to say that it all goes back
To my persuading the angry man I was,
Alone in prison, to set aside, after ten years,
The metaphor of life as a battle
And take up, for the second half of my bid,
The metaphor of a voyage.
But you're only guessing, as I would be,
If you try to say how I did it.

No doubt my struggle in prison
Not to blame others for my behavior
Helps to explain my success in prodding
Others to accept their responsibility.
No doubt I said on one of your visits,
"The day I forget the man I killed
Is the day I begin to die." But it's also true
I had to forgive myself enough,
After years of gloom, to take the courses
That let me graduate from the prison college.
And who can say how I managed it,
How, while holding on to the past, I let go?

I'm only guessing myself. Yes, I can tell you,
To borrow your figure, that something urged me
To grab the tiller and hoist my sail,
Some glimpse of a future glimmering near the horizon.
But who knows how I recognized it as mine,

Mine to have if I made an effort to reach it,
When it seemed so distant,
So far from the life I'd known before?

in memory of John Hemmers

Not the End

Don't let the quarreling near the end
Convince you the breakup would have been predictable
From the beginning to somebody more insightful.

Remember that any suggestion back then
Of the actual outcome would have been swept aside
By the evidence that the joys you shared
With your beloved would prove enduring:
The joy on workdays of cooking supper together,
The joy on weekends of rambling the woods
With no agenda.

The silences weren't a sign of holding back.
They were calm and easy, your thoughts
Drifting away on a stream of association
And then returning with a sprig of woodland flowers.
Here, this is for you, each said, and meant it.

And remember the climb you loved, to the ridge,
The wide view of the valley that left you both
Feeling open to whatever the day might offer.

Don't diminish those moments now by wondering
What you could have done to make them last
Had you been attentive enough to cherish them.
You were happy back then, remember,
And knew you were happy.

What you need now isn't the work
Of regret but the work of gratitude.
And all it takes to be grateful is to feel grateful.

Go back to the beginning and embrace its bounty.
Beneath the story of cause and consequence
Another story is pointing another way.

Carl Dennis is the author of eleven previous works of poetry, as well as a collection of essays, *Poetry as Persuasion*. A recipient of the Ruth Lilly Prize and the Pulitzer Prize, he lives in Buffalo, New York.

JOHN ASHBERY
Selected Poems
Self-Portrait in a Convex
  Mirror

TED BERRIGAN
The Sonnets

LAUREN BERRY
The Lifting Dress

JOE BONOMO
Installations

PHILIP BOOTH
Selves

JULIANNE BUCHSBAUM
The Apothecary's Heir

JIM CARROLL
Fear of Dreaming:
  The Selected Poems
Living at the Movies
Void of Course

ALISON HAWTHORNE
DEMING
Genius Loci
Rope

CARL DENNIS
Another Reason
Callings
New and Selected Poems
  1974–2004
Practical Gods
Ranking the Wishes
Unknown Friends

DIANE DI PRIMA
Loba

STUART DISCHELL
Backwards Days
Dig Safe

STEPHEN DOBYNS
Velocities: New and Selected
  Poems, 1966–1992

EDWARD DORN
Way More West: New and
  Selected Poems

ROGER FANNING
The Middle Ages

ADAM FOULDS
The Broken Word

CARRIE FOUNTAIN
Burn Lake

AMY GERSTLER
Crown of Weeds: Poems
Dearest Creature
Ghost Girl
Medicine
Nerve Storm

EUGENE GLORIA
Drivers at the Short-Time
  Motel
Hoodlum Birds
My Favorite Warlord

DEBORA GREGER
By Herself
Desert Fathers, Uranium
  Daughters
God
Men, Women, and Ghosts
Western Art

TERRANCE HAYES
Hip Logic
Lighthead
Wind in a Box

NATHAN HOKS
The Narrow Circle

ROBERT HUNTER
Sentinel and Other Poems

MARY KARR
Viper Rum

WILLIAM KECKLER
Sanskrit of the Body

JACK KEROUAC
Book of Sketches
Book of Blues
Book of Haikus

JOANNA KLINK
Circadian
Raptus

JOANNE KYGER
As Ever: Selected Poems

ANN LAUTERBACH
Hum
If in Time:
  Selected Poems, 1975–
  2000
On a Stair
Or to Begin Again
Under the Sign

CORINNE LEE
PYX

PHILLIS LEVIN
May Day
Mercury

WILLIAM LOGAN
Macbeth in Venice
Madame X
Strange Flesh
The Whispering Gallery

ADRIAN MATEJKA
The Big Smoke
Mixology

MICHAEL MCCLURE
Huge Dreams:
  San Francisco and Beat
  Poems

DAVID MELTZER
David's Copy:
  The Selected Poems of
  David Meltzer

ROBERT MORGAN
Terroir

CAROL MUSKE-DUKES
An Octave Above Thunder
Red Trousseau
Twin Cities

ALICE NOTLEY
Culture of One
The Descent of Alette
Disobedience
In the Pines
Mysteries of Small Houses

WILLIE PERDOMO
The Essential Hits of Shorty
  Bon Bon

LAWRENCE RAAB
The History of Forgetting
Visible Signs: New and
  Selected Poems

BARBARA RAS
The Last Skin
One Hidden Stuff

MICHAEL ROBBINS
Alien vs. Predator

PATTIANN ROGERS
Generations
Holy Heathen Rhapsody
Wayfare

WILLIAM STOBB
Absentia
Nervous Systems

TRYFON TOLIDES
An Almost Pure Empty
  Walking

ANNE WALDMAN
Gossamurmur
Kill or Cure
Manatee/Humanity
Structure of the World
  Compared to a Bubble

JAMES WELCH
Riding the Earthboy 40

PHILIP WHALEN
Overtime: Selected Poems

ROBERT WRIGLEY
Anatomy of Melancholy and
  Other Poems
Beautiful Country
Earthly Meditations: New
  and Selected Poems
Lives of the Animals
Reign of Snakes

MARK YAKICH
The Importance of Peeling
  Potatoes in Ukraine
Unrelated Individuals
  Forming a Group Waiting
  to Cross

JOHN YAU
Borrowed Love Poems
Paradiso Diaspora